IMAGES
of England

CASTLEFORD

Castleford Co-operative Women's Guild c.1890-1900. No names are known but it is thought that some members of the Atack family are in the group.

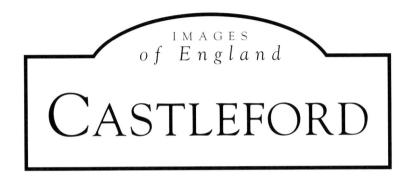

IMAGES
of England

CASTLEFORD

From the collection of
Wakefield Metropolitan District Library Service

TEMPUS

First published 1994
Reprinted 1999, 2004

Tempus Publishing Limited
The Mill, Brimscombe Port,
Stroud, Gloucestershire, GL5 2QG
www.tempus-publishing.com

British Library Cataloguing in Publication Data.
A catalogue record for this book is available from the British Library.

ISBN 0 7524 0047 9

Typesetting and origination by Tempus Publishing Limited.
Printed in Great Britain.

Contents

Introduction   6

1.   Buildings   9

2.   In and Around the Town   13

3.   Shopping   31

4.   The Working Town   49

5.   Coal-getting   61

6.   Around the River   73

7.   History on the Move   81

8.   Housing   91

9.   Schooldays   99

10.   Sport   105

11.   Special Events   113

12.   Leisure Time   121

13.   At Peace and War   133

14.   Airedale and Fryston   141

15.   Glasshoughton   149

Acknowledgements   160

A travelling ice-cream man with a group of children c.1930's, possibly in the potteries area of Whitwood Mere.

Introduction

Between the 1820's and the end of the nineteenth century Castleford changed from a small agricultural village which stood on the site of the Roman fort of Lagentium to an overcrowded industrial town.

As a result, it experienced all the medical and social problems that rapid industrial expansion and population growth bring. No longer was the old ditty about the two Castleford rivers – 'Castleford ladies must needs be fair, for they wash in Calder and rinse in Aire' – true.

Whilst fine villas with gardens (later to be built over by tightly packed roadside shops) were springing up in the town centre, street upon street of dwellings, mostly of poor quality, were rapidly being built to accommodate the large influx of population which came to work in the mining, pottery, glass, chemical, brick, iron and other labour-intensive industries which had started up in the town. At one time the town had the unenviable distinction of being the 'most populated square mile of England'.

Gradually attempts were made to improve conditions, a municipal cemetery was opened and the small graveyard around the parish church was closed. A new water supply was being laid, elementary schools were built, gas was introduced and streets around the town centre were paved and lit.

In the early years of the twentieth century an electric tram system was introduced (later superseded by buses) which complemented the existing rail system. Among other additions were the public library which opened in 1905 and a secondary school, which was mostly fee paying with some scholarship places. This school provided a higher level of education than the elementary schools. Three of its pupils in the early years were Henry Moore, the sculptor, and his friends Arthur Dalby (who became HM Inspector of Art in Schools) and the artist and theatrical designer Albert Wainwright.

In the 1920's and 1930's Castleford was enlarged to include Whitwood and Whitwood Mere, Glasshoughton, parts of Allerton Bywater (from the river to the canal), and part of the parish of Ferry Fryston plus New Fryston. New housing estates were built (mainly after the Second World War).

The depressions of the 1920's and 1930's affected Castleford badly because of its reliance on industry and Breffitt's glass works, closed in 1926. In addition the town suffered two more catastrophes – the Market Hall fire of 31 December 1927 and a terrible explosion at the Chemical works of Hickson & Welch on 4 July 1930.

In 1929 the Princess Mary opened the rebuilt Market Hall along with a new hospital and the War Memorial Maternity Home.

From the 1950's onwards traditional industries declined and disappeared, leaving no collieries, glassworks, brickworks or potteries in the town.

Town centre redevelopment schemes of the 1960s led to the demolition of many pre-Victorian and Victorian buildings; the Victorian railway station was demolished and the present station has now been replaced by a shelter on account of the severe curtailment of the railway system.

After being a Local Board, an Urban District Council and eventually a Borough (in 1955), the town finally lost its independence and became part of the Wakefield Metropolitan District in 1974.

Over the years Castleford Library has amassed a collection of over 2,000 photographs. Many were donated or loaned for copying by generous individuals, who photographed buildings prior to demolition, or rescued old photographs and postcards, depositing them with the library, thus ensuring that present and future generations would have a visual record of the town's past.

It has been a difficult task to select photographs for this book. We have tried to be true to the memory of the Castleford that has gone, neither romanticising nor denigrating it.

Colleen Rawlinson
Christine Wadsworth
Anne Farrington

Carlton Street at night in the 1950's. The Carlton Hotel is now the Carlton and the pub next door – The Royal Engineer – is shops.

One
Buildings

Castleford Library, one of many public libraries financed by the benefactor Andrew Carnegie, opened in 1905 in Carlton Street.

All Saints, Castleford Parish Church. There has been a church on this site since the twelfth century. This building was replaced by the present church in 1868.

The old rectory, Rectory Street, close to the Parish Church. This ancient building, reputed to pre-date Stuart times, was demolished some time after 1898.

The old Castleford town hall, which stood close to the site of the present day Civic Centre. Originally called Redhill House, it was occupied by the town's M.P. Sir John Austin and his family. Belgian refugees were billeted here in the First World War.

A side view of the town hall showing later extensions, photographed by the late David Jagger shortly before its demolition.

The court house, Jessop Street, was opened in 1897. The building was later changed to a police station to replace the one which had previously been located at the top of Bradley Street.

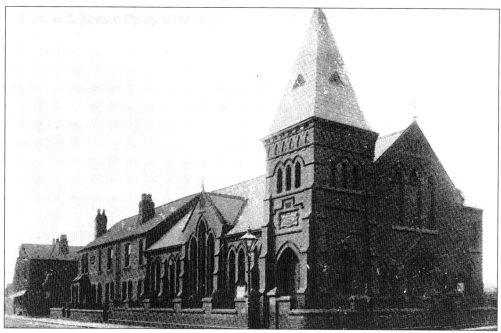

Whitwood Mere Memorial Church was a Methodist church opened on 26 July 1899 and closed at the end of February 1963 because of declining congregations. Later the building was used as a car salesroom.

Two
In and Around Town

Albion Street c.1900, showing Hardy's Printers and C. Smith, Coal Dealer and Carting Agent.

Station Road at the junction of Carlton Street and Bank Street in the early 1900's. The shops on the right are now the YEB showrooms. At one time NEGAS also had a showroom next door.

Carlton Street at the junction of Commercial Street, probably before 1906 as there are no tram posts and the buildings on the left are private houses and not shops.

A similar view to the preceding photograph, taken several years later. Tram posts can be seen on the right and the private houses on the left have become shops. The turrets of Carlton Street Methodist Church can be seen.

Carlton Street Methodist Church, which stood on the spot now occupied by G.T. Smith & Sons' supermarket and adjoining shops. The building adjacent to it was also demolished to make way for the development.

Carlton Street at the junction of Bank Street and Station Road *c.*1910. The building on the left is now Barclay's Bank (formerly a branch of the famous bank of Leatham & Tew).

Carlton Street in the era of the trams (1906-1929), showing the Co-operative building (now replaced by Leo's, which changed its name to Pioneer in 1994).

Carlton Street in the 1950's. This section of the street was pedestrianised in 1994.

Carlton Street c.1976. The building in the foreground was replaced by a branch of the Halifax Building Society in 1991.

Carlton Street at night during the late 1950's, at its junction with Albert Street.

Carlton Street at night in the 1950's, near the junction with Bradley Street.

Carlton Street during the late 1950's viewed from Mercer's pram and toy shop, at the junction with Albert Street.

Carlton Lanes car park now occupies the site of these shops in Bridge Street which were demolished in 1964.

Bridge Street, looking towards the Ship Inn and the lamp in the early 1900's.

Bridge Street *c.*1910, looking towards the junction with Carlton Street.

Photograph of the lamp at the 'Bridge Foot' which acted as a meeting place, a gathering point for parades and a forum for public meetings. It was demolished c.1964.

Bridge Street in the early 1900's, looking towards the Ship Inn and the lamp.

Carlton Street at the junction with Bridge Street c.1910-1920. The buildings and shops on the left were demolished in the 1960s as part of the Castleway shops scheme.

Bridge Street at the junction of Carlton Street in the 1970's. The Keel Inn and Miners Arms were demolished as part of the Aire Street-Bridge Street widening scheme in 1977. In 1979 the weathervane over the Miners Arms was re-erected at Whitwood College.

Bridge Street, 1972. The first three shops on the left were demolished as part of the 1977 road widening scheme.

The junction of Aire Street and Bridge Street *c.*1910.

Aire Street at the junction of Sagar Street, 1908. Some of the buildings were demolished as part of the Aire Street-Bridge Street road widening scheme of 1977.

Aire Street c.1908 when it was a busy shopping area.

The junction of Albion Street, Carlton Street and Church Street c.1900. Hardy's Printers on the right moved from Aire Street to Albion Street in 1894, and was demolished in 1964.

The same view taken in the 1970's.

Church Street at the junction of Carlton Street *c*.1910. This was a busy shopping area at this time.

Church Street in the 1970's. The property on the left was demolished to make way for the Aire Street-Bridge Street road widening scheme.

Smawthorne Lane *c.*1900.

Smawthorne Lane *c.*1900.

Healdfield Road c.1900, originally known as Cemetery Road.

Park Road, now Ferrybridge Road. Vale Royd is now Breadalbane Residential Home.

Three

Shopping

Market Hall re-opening by Princess Mary in August 1929, after being destroyed by the fire of 31 December 1927. This photograph shows the side entrance to the open market from the dry goods market.

Castleford Co-operative Society Ltd, Carlton Street, built towards the end of the nineteenth century. It was replaced by a Leo's (now Pioneer) supermarket in the 1980's.

Castleford Co-operative Industrial Society Ltd, which opened in 1908 on the junction of Carlton Street and Station Road.

The Toll Hill branch of the Castleford Co-operative Industrial Society Ltd, at the junction of Holywell Lane and Fryston Road. At present it is a video rental shop.

The Whitwood Mere branch of the Castleford Industrial Society Ltd, opened in 1903.

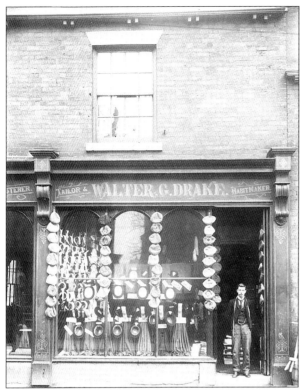

Walter G. Drake, tailor and
outfitter of Carlton Street,
probably 1892.

Stein's pork butchers, established in Castleford
at the close of the nineteenth century. The
shop suffered damage during the First World
War as a result of anti-German fervour.

Rickard's grocery shop was a family business established in Castleford in the mid nineteenth century. This photograph was probably taken during the First World War.

Shop assistant Alice Haslam outside Jackson's Ltd, gentleman's outfitters on Bridge Street c.1920.

Shepherds grocery shop, Carlton Street, *c.*1920's.

Nicholls, jewellers and silversmiths in Aire Street, *c*.1920. They later moved to Carlton Street.

The Globe Tea Co. grocers were established in the early 1880's in Aire Street. The property was demolished to make way for the Aire Street-Bridge Street scheme of 1977.

A. Lightowler, greengrocers of Castleford and Pontefract during the early decade of the century. This shop stood on Aire Street, and later became Mitchell's, which sold artists materials and religious statuettes. It was demolished to make way for the Aire Street-Bridge Street scheme.

Gallons Ltd, grocers, were a familiar sight in local towns. Castleford's branch was located in Bridge Street from c.1900.

Clarence Brumwell, the manager, and his wife outside the Army Stores, Bradley Street, *c.*1920.

Meadow Dairy in Carlton Street, 1918. Pictured are William Baxter and Mrs Mary Jane Hardy, née Long.

Rogers and Sons were established in Albion Street, Castleford, *c*.1875.

Allpass & Co. Ltd of Carlton Street *c*.1900. They moved to Bank Street in the 1920's.

Rodger's bike shop was a familiar landmark at the junction of Bridge Street, Ferrybridge Road and Pontefract Road.

The shop owned by Joseph Chadwick on Front Street, Glasshoughton.

Dodsworth & Sons, cabinet makers, who occupied premises in Carlton Street, Bradley Street, Rectory Street and Bridge Street in the decades before and after 1900.

Parkin's ironmongers was established in 1908 and expanded from the corner of Bank Street and Aire Street into Bradley Street. For many years the key above the door was a famous Castleford landmark. The shop was demolished in the 1970's.

Shop owned by J. Fletcher at Churchfields, Glasshoughton, c.1910.

Carlton Street, looking towards Bridge Street in the 1960's. Redmans the grocers can be seen on the right. Scarrs sold all kinds of household goods.

The open market on Carlton Street, next to the library, in the 1950's. The Spencer Centre now stands on the site.

Carlton Street in 1955, showing the public library and Market Hall. Over the years many Castleford couples met under the Market Hall clock.

The Market Hall, which was restored in 1929 following the fire of 31 December 1927. Trading ceased in August 1991 and demolition followed in 1992. The shell of the arcade still remains.

The open market after the fire of 31 December 1927.

An interior view of the Market Hall after the fire of 31 December 1927.

Four

The Working Town

The beehive kilns of Clokies Pottery stood on the site of the original pottery established by the renowned David Dunderdale in the late eighteenth century. The pottery had several owners before it closed in 1961.

Clokies Pottery – the handling shop, from a brochure of publicity photographs published by the firm.

A worker at a local pottery works.

Clokies Pottery – the biscuit oven from the same publicity brochure as above.

An aerial view (undated) looking over Church Street and out to Whitwood Mere. Clokies Pottery kilns are in the top left of the photograph. This photograph shows the crowded buildings of old Castleford, and its dirty, fume-laden atmosphere.

Allinsons Flour Mill c.1961, showing the swirls of foam blown from the river.

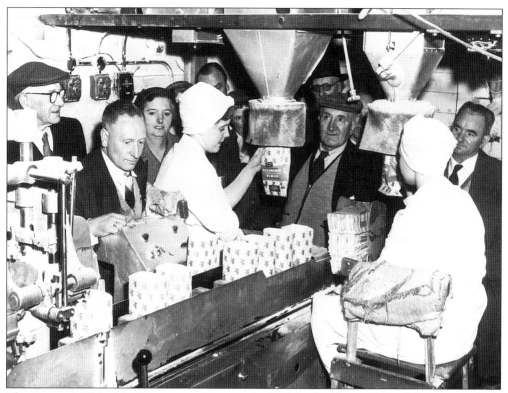

The Queens Mill in Aire Street was taken over in 1921 by the National Food Company, which had been established by Thomas Allinson. The flour is being put into bags during an open day c.1950.

Castleford Co-operative Industrial Society Ltd bakery, possibly in the 1930's.

Church Street *c.*1926, looking towards the Lock Lane area. Note the crowded nature of the housing jostling with commercial and industrial premises. Many of these buildings were demolished in the 1970s. Excavations of some of the sites revealed much information about Castleford's Roman past.

Wood yard owned by Richard Cliffe and Son, established 1856, boat builders, and English and foreign timber merchants.

A wood yard (probably Richard Cliffe and Son's), showing the horses which provided much of the power for industry in the Victorian and Edwardian eras.

A group of workmen from Breffitt's Glassworks. The little boys were known as 'taker inners'; their sole job was to wait until the glass blowers had blown a shape, then take the molten glass on a long forked pole to the 'lehr' (furnace).

A group of glass blowers (probably at Breffitts). So much force was used by the blowers that from time to time their cheeks ruptured and they would be laid off work for some weeks at a time.

House building in 1930. Second and third from left are James Widdop Snr and James Widdop Jnr.

Men at work outside the Co-operative Retail Society in Carlton Street *c*. the 1950's. This building stood on the site now occupied by the Pioneer supermarket.

A rare photograph of men at work constructing a culvert sometime in the 1950's – without safety helmets!

Curious about the photographer, a group gathers at the mineral water works of T. Smith.

A serious explosion at the Hickson & Welch site in 1930 killed 13 men. The works were destroyed and many families were rendered homeless. It was reported that windows were shattered as far away as Methley.

Tarsprayers employed by Whitwood Urban District Council c.1926. Left to right: J. Bourne, J. Tonks (who took many of the photographs in this book and became the Mayor of Castleford's chauffeur), T. Wright.

Opposite: Castleford Fire Brigade. As fire fighting equipment grew in size and sophistication, the Brigade required larger accommodation. They occupied premises in Carlton Street close to the library; later they moved to Sagar Street, then to Smawthorne Lane, and finally to their present site on Beancroft Road.

Workmen employed by Whitwood Urban District Council c.1920. Note the message on the tailgate of the lorry.

Five
Coal-Getting

The once-familiar silhouette of Glasshoughton Colliery, opened in 1869 and closed in 1986.

Wheldale Colliery was established in 1868 by Dr Holt and closed in 1987. A strike between 1902 and 1904 lasted 68 weeks. The rescue team helped at the Lofthouse Colliery disaster in 1973.

Wheldale Colliery viewed from the railway line.

Coal picking, probably at Wheldale Colliery during the strike of 1912.

Pit ponies were treasured and cared for in the mines. New recruits to the mines were often guided by the ponies, who knew every roadway and junction underground.

Wheldale Colliery, which closed in 1987. A single-decker bus can be seen on Wheldon Lane, which divided the colliery into two. The colliery railway crossed Wheldon Lane and traffic had to be stopped to allow engines to pass over it.

Fryston Colliery, showing the distinctive pit headgear which was demolished in October 1987 (the colliery having closed in December 1985).

Fryston Colliery, showing part of the bus turning circle outside the colliery baths – this being the only bus stop in Fryston village.

Fryston Colliery, showing the gantry and pit headgear, possibly sometime in the 1930's. The colliery was sunk in the 1870's and Fryston village was built to house the miners in 1890. From 15 October 1902 to January 1904, Fryston and Wheldale miners took part in the 68 week strike.

Opposite: Fryston Colliery baths, which were installed in the 1930's.

A pit pony at the mining training centre, Whitwood Colliery.

An aerial view of Glasshoughton Colliery, showing the network of railway lines which served the colliery. Rows of houses adjacent to the colliery can also be seen.

Glasshoughton Colliery, showing the pit headgear.

The coking plant at Glasshoughton, owned by the Yorkshire Coking and Chemical Company. In the foreground lorries are being filled – note the separate compartments for the different grades of coke.

Whitwood Colliery before 1900, showing the headgear and railway lines.

Whitwood Colliery c.1935, showing the gantry and tubs on the colliery railway. This and the above photograph appeared in a publicity booklet promoting Briggs' Collieries.

N.U.M. galas were preceded by a procession and parade of colliery banners. This one took place in Castleford in 1964.

Six
Around the River

Floods in Bridge Street c.1976. The River Aire frequently burst its banks before the development of flood defences.

Floods in Princess Street, 1932.

Aire Street in the floods of September 1946. Food rations were destroyed when the floodwater entered homes, and boats from Pontefract Park were used to rescue families. Note the new Star Cinema, which is now demolished.

Hickson & Welch in the floods of September 1946.

Bridge Street, near the junction with Carlton Street (possibly in the 1950's or early '60's), with lanterns to mark the edge of the causeway during the night. The four shops on the left were demolished as part of the 1977 road development scheme, the building on the right being demolished in 1964.

Foam building up under the bridge over the River Aire c.1961.

Foam on the River Aire at the back of Aire Street, 1961.

Aire Street, 1961. Between the 1950's and 1970's scouring agents deposited in the Rivers Aire and Calder from the heavy woollen districts were churned into soapsuds when they reached the weir at Castleford. Castlefordians dreaded windy days – the slightest breeze would send 'snowstorms' of suds over Aire Street, Wheldon Road and Bridge Street, damaging clothing and car paintwork. Several schemes were employed to solve the problem, the most successful of which involved spraying the suds as they reached the weir.

This is thought to be a photograph of Hunt Brothers Chemical Works and wharf on the River Aire c.1900. They manufactured Sulphate of Soda, Sulphuric Acid and Chloride of Lime.

The weir and Allinsons flour mill, adjacent to extensive riverside development along the banks of the River Aire, in 1931.

Clokies Pottery as seen from the River Calder during the 1950's-60's.

Castleford Bridge, built by Jesse Hartley in 1808, viewed from the ruins of an old mill which has long since disappeared.

Castleford Bridge leading to Lock Lane, which was part of Allerton Bywater until the 1930's. To the left, partly obscured by the bridge, is Bridge Foot House, which stood on the site of what was Hoptons garage.

A close-up view of Bridge Foot House.

Seven
History on the Move

Excavation work on the Aire & Calder Canal.

Maintenance on the canal at Bulholme Lock in 1976.

Tugs moored on the canal by the lock-keepers houses. In the background can be seen the iron railway bridge.

Barges moored on the River Aire at Castleford. In the background is the parish church of All Saints.

Mobile shop owned by Cllr John Kirkby, in Fryston Road, Airedale – possibly in the 1930's.

Horse drawn transport for the Mothers Union trip *c.*1900. Unlike the present time, all the women are wearing hats and even the babies are wearing bonnets.

Castleford's first railway station was opened in 1840 in Bridge Street. It was superseded in the 1870's by the main station and demolished in the 1960's.

Cutsyke station closed in 1968. It was originally owned by the Lancashire and Yorkshire Railway Company.

Cutsyke level crossing before the First World War.

A commercial lorry advertising S.P. Sanders Coal & Coke Dealer, Townville, and showing the product range of the Yorkshire Coking & Chemical Co. Ltd, Castleford.

A beer tanker struggling to deliver its load at the junction of Carlton Street and Bridge Street in the September floods of 1946.

Driver and clippie pose in front of their decorated tram for Castleford Carnival, probably in the 1920's.

A tram inspection, Pontefract Road, Castleford. The tramways in Castleford opened on 29 October 1906. Unable to withstand the competition from the newly emerging bus companies, the trams stopped running in 1925, the last tram being the 11 p.m. from Pontefract to the Keel Inn at Castleford on 1 November 1925.

A charabanc *c.* the 1920's.

Night time at the bus station, Albion Street, thought to have been photographed shortly after its opening in May 1963.

A single-decker bus of the West Riding Auto Company, with a Castleford route destination. Its driver and conductor pose proudly alongside.

Eight
Housing

The cutting of the 'Park Hill' in 1947, to provide direct access to the planned housing estates in Airedale. Before it was cut, all traffic, even buses, used the narrow, winding Red Hill (named from the colour of its top layer, which, legend states, was due to dried blood from a long-ago battle).

An undated photograph, possibly of one of the old yards, showing some of the poor housing conditions prevalent in Victorian times and after. Very few photographs of this type of housing have survived.

Wellington Street in the 1930's, before it was re-paved.

Victoria Place stood at the bottom of the open market off Aire Street. The two ladies are Eva and Elsie Lapidge, who ran the 'Penny Stall' in Castleford Market for fifty-six and thirty-eight years respectively. This photograph was taken as they left their home for the last time in 1956, shortly before demolition.

Barnes Road, Castleford *c.*1900.

Albion Street *c.*1910, showing terrace housing and shops intermingled.

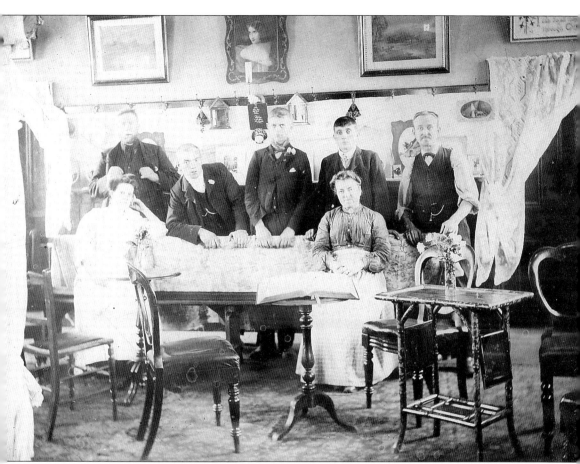

Interior view of Harvey's Farm, Glasshoughton, 1880-90's. It stood opposite the Malt Shovel public house on Front Street and was demolished in the 1980's.

The birthplace of world-famous sculptor Henry Moore, photographed by the late David Jagger in 1971. It was later demolished.

British Industrial Steel Frame (BISF) houses being constructed in Queens Park Drive in 1947 as part of the Redhill No. 2 scheme which was completed in 1949.

A close-up of one of the houses under construction.

Newly built houses in Queens Park Drive.

West Mead, built and ready for occupation. Prefabricated houses were a temporary solution to the post-war housing shortage, but lasted for many more years than was envisaged at the time of construction.

Nine
Schooldays

A class of boys at Pontefract Road School c.1910.

Welbeck Street Schools viewed from the church tower in 1968. The original infants' school part was demolished in 1974; the boys' school was used as a storeroom and demolished some years later.

Welbeck Street Schools c.1900. The foundation stone was laid in 1877 for what was originally the girls' school; to the left was the boys' school, which was built in 1894.

Teaching staff at Welbeck Street School, thought to have been photographed in the early 1900's. The young girls at the front are pupil teachers.

Welbeck Street School c.1908, when Mrs Louisa Wood was the mistress of the infants' school.

Welbeck Street School Choir, 1927.

Wesleyan School, 1902. The school was built in 1857. In 1904 the chief architect to the West Riding County Council reported that the buildings were 'generally old and dilapidated'.

Pontefract Road Board School pupils c.1910.

A group of boys from the same school in the 1920's-30's.

Whitwood Mere Infants School, now designated a listed building. Oliver Hill designed the school to provide each classroom with full open access to the garden area. Opened in 1941 with murals by John Skeaping, the school closed in 1993, a truly unique building which continues to attract attention.

The opening day of the above school. The man with the moustache is Ezra Taylor, who became Castleford's first mayor in 1955.

Ten
Sport

Castleford Hornets Rugby Union team around the 1890's. From left to right, back row: -?-, -?-, A. Starks, D. Walton, -?-, -?-, J. Hartley. Middle row: A. Hanson, -?-, T. Needham, Speed, -?-, -?-, -?-. Front row: R. Hanson, -?-, Johnson, -?-.

Castleford Football Club, 1896.

Castleford Town Association Football Club, 1913-14 season. From left to right, top row: W. Ambler (Pres), H. Cranswick, Lockyer, Ward, Ponds, Batty, Tierrey, G. Burton (Director), W. Leggitt (Trainer). Middle row: Huxford, Woodward, Robins, Abrams, Charles. Front row: Baines, Graham, Martin.

A photographic memento of a YMCA outing c.1930. Motorcyclying and bicycling was very popular between the wars and just after the Second World War. Whole families would ride to the coast for a day out and many cycling clubs were formed.

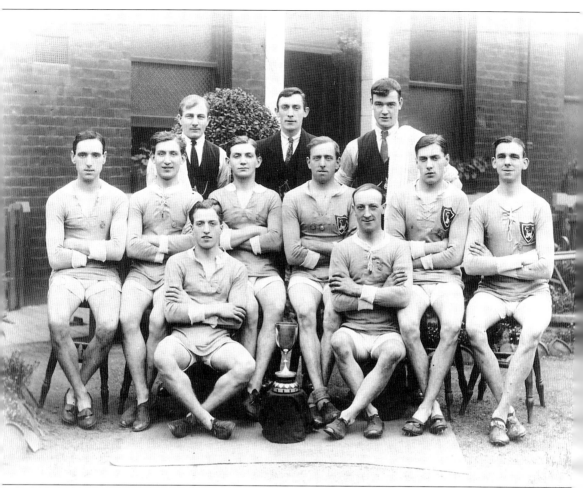

Castleford Hornets, 1919-20 season, winners of the Leeds & District Cross Country Championship (Junior Harriers race). Back row: G. Taylor (Trainer), T. Liversedge (Secretary), H. Lorriman (Trainer). Middle row: G. Blewell, F. Armitage, E. Armitage, F. Brown (Capt & individual champion), W. Brown, E. Gardiner. Front row: H. Newbold, J. Turner.

Castleford Anglers' Society in the 1930's.

Whitwood Cricket Club c.1907.

Yorkshire County player Herbert Sutcliffe at Castleford Cricket Club, 1928.

Arthur 'Bruss' Atkinson, captain of the Castleford Rugby League team, winners of the 1935 Challenge Cup. Mr Atkinson later became manager of the New Star cinema. He died in 1963.

Castleford Rugby League team, 1935 cup winners. From top row, left to right: Crossley, Nowells, McManus, Sadler, Smith, Taylor. Middle row: Gideon Shaw, Hailey, Lewis, Croston, Askin, Rhodes, Pickles. Front row: Cunniffe, Adams, Atkinson, Davis, England.

Princess Street, Wheldon Lane, in May 1935, decorated to welcome home the Rugby League Challenge Cup Final winners.

Some of the Castleford Rugby League team who won the Challenge Cup in 1970. Left to right: B. Kirkbride, I. Stenton, T. Briggs, K. Hepworth, C. Dickinson, A. Hardisty, T. Thomas, M. Redfearn and B. Lockwood, with M. Reilly in the background. Players not shown: D. Edwards, A. Lownes and D. Hartley. Subs were D. Hargrave and S. Norton.

Glasshoughton Colliery Rugby League team, 1937-38. Social welfare clubs at many collieries ran their own football, rugby league and cricket teams.

Eleven
Special Events

A Sunday School procession files along Aire Street, past the lamp, c.1906.

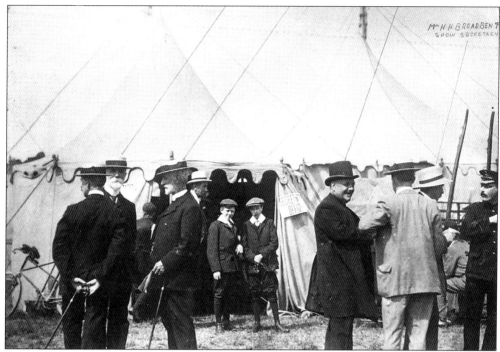

Castleford Flower Show *c*.1890. Mr J. Simpson J.P., Rev. R. Gardner-Smith, Rector of Castleford, Rev. B. Hemsworth and Mr H.H. Broadbent, Show Secretary, are pictured.

Princess Marie Louise arriving to open the Parish Church bazaar in 1914. She is welcomed by Canon Hewitt, Mr F.S. Hatchard and Lady Wheeler.

The opening of Castleford & Normanton District Hospital by the Princess Mary, 23 August 1929. It was financed by weekly collections in factories and mines, fund raising events and gifts from private individuals. Castlefordians have always had a great affection for this hospital. Over the years fund raising events have been held to buy equipment and furnishings (many by the Hospital Comforts Fund). Nowadays it deals with psychiatric and geriatric nursing, the surgical and casualty departments having been transferred to Pontefract Infirmary.

Another photograph of the Princess Mary opening the Castleford & Normanton District Hospital.

Charter Day, 30 July 1955. Castleford received its charter to become a borough on that day. Ezra Taylor, the first mayor, can be seen introducing the Mayoress, his daughter Mrs Olive Stokes, to the Princess Royal.

Castleford Trades Council, 1936.

Bellamy's carnival float, which won first prize in the Castleford Carnival of 1963. This confectionery firm began in the 1900's and in 1964 it was taken over by John Mackintosh, later becoming Rowntree Mackintosh. It is now Nestlé.

Glasshoughton & Castleford Collieries Ltd Haulage Signal Display float, entitled 'snap time', probably for Miners Pageant c.1925.

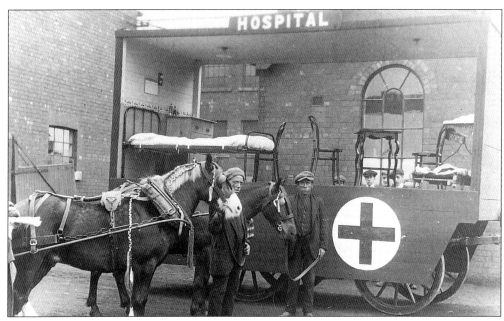

Another float probably for the same pageant.

The event shown is believed to be a party held in the Drill Hall to celebrate the 1953 coronation.

Launching of the Bookmobile in May 1950 by Cllr Mrs Dodsworth. It was a converted single-decker bus which toured Whitwood, Glasshoughton, Airedale and Fryston for many years.

Alderman Ezra Taylor in 1955, when he became the first mayor of Castleford.

'Taws', or marble competitions, were popular inter-town events. A challenge match between Castleford and the BSA factory, Birmingham, was held in Birmingham in 1955. Sir Bernard and Lady Docker were guests at this occasion, and also visited Castleford.

Sculptor Henry Moore was given the Freedom of the Borough of Castleford on 29 June 1962, along with Jesse Dowding JP. From left to right: Jesse Dowding, the mayor Alderman (later Sir) Jack Smart, Henry Moore and Ernest Hutchinson, the Town Clerk.

Twelve

Leisure Time

Castleford Amusement Proprietors and Managers effort for local charities, 5 February 1921.

The Queens Theatre, known variously as the Queens Hall and the Hippodrome. Latterly it became the Queens Cinema and, finally, ASDA supermarket. Opened in 1899, it housed variety shows, circuses, silent and talking pictures and Bingo. It was demolished in 1990 as part of the Carlton Lanes development.

Mr and Mrs Gilligan travelled through the local area giving roundabout rides in exchange for jam jars or rags. One of their horse drawn rides was sold to York Castle Museum, and another has been at Kirkstall Abbey Museum since 1979. Mr Gilligan died in 1977.

THE KIOSK CAFE,

CASTLEFORD.

Kiosk Cafe, Sykes Street, was a popular venue for social gatherings.

Castleford & District Division of the St John Ambulance Brigade. These members were on duty for the royal visit to Leeds on 7 July 1908.

Pit Pony Show c.1950. On the left is Ezra Taylor.

The first motor car in Castleford, Mr T. Gill at the wheel. Mr Gill was the owner of Castleford's Providence Pottery.

The exterior of the Florence Street swimming baths. Opened on 31 May 1911, the baths closed in 1979 and were demolished in 1980.

DEEP END
7.FEET

An interior view of the baths.

Florence Street baths transformed into the Festival Hall. Every year, after the summer swimming season, the pool was drained and boarded over, and the baths became the Festival Hall, where events such as dances, concerts and the 'Taws' championships were held.

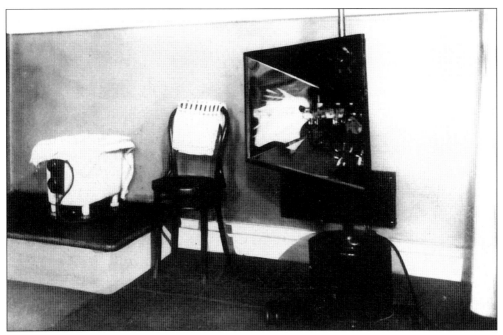

The Sun-ray room at the Florence Street baths c.1947.

The Co-operative Hall, which was used for entertainments, exhibitions and private functions, was the first floor of the Co-operative store which stood on the site of the present day Pioneer supermarket.

View from Queens Park overlooking Ferrybridge Road c.1900, showing fewer houses than at the present day. Victoria Park was opened in 1897 for Queen Victoria's Diamond Jubilee. The land was donated by two local landowners – the Earl of Crewe and John Davison Bland. It later became known as Queens Park.

The entrance to Queens Park *c.*1960.

Queens Park, showing the bandstand *c.*1905.

A close-up of the bandstand c.1905.

Redhill, looking over to Queens Park in the early 1900's.

The Valley Gardens in 1969. Recently the play area and shelter were given a face-lift as part of the Smawthorne Urban Renewal Scheme.

Another view of the Valley Gardens.

Thirteen

At Peace and War

Castleford Co-operative Industrial Society Ltd Roll of Honour, 1914-1918.

Castleford Subscription Prize Band toured Germany in 1913. Names from top left to bottom right: Garbutt, Westmoreland, Nelson, Stokes, Sewell, Jourdain, Bromwich, Titterton, Allison, Prust, Beadle, Voelkel, Andrews, Sanderson, Shooter, Thorpe, Simpson, Belcher, Turner, Huntington, Pickering, Polunham, Pickersgill, Williams, Stamp, Prince, Garbutt, Atherton.

Princess Marie Louise opening the Parish Church bazaar in 1914.

Lilian Dexter, a munitions worker in the First World War, one of many women who worked in the munitions factories. The work could be dangerous, and in 1916 an explosion at the Barnbow factory in Leeds killed thirty-five women, including four Castleford women – Mary Gibson, Polly Brown, Eliza Grant and Edith Levitt.

Lance-corporal Thomas Bryan VC, 1882-1945. A resident of Whitwood Mere, he was awarded the Victoria Cross in 1917 for single-handedly knocking out a German machine-gun post at Arras. He is buried at Arksey Cemetery. In 1972 a commemorative plaque was placed in Castleford Civic Centre. Bryan Close at Whitwood Mere was named in his honour.

Peace Procession in Carlton Street, 1918. On the left can be seen the Co-operative stores which stood on the site now occupied by the Pioneer supermarket.

The Princess Mary opening the War Memorial Maternity Home, 23 August 1929. In one day she opened the maternity home, Castleford & Normanton District Hospital and the rebuilt Market Hall.

The War Memorial Maternity Home. Originally a private house, it was converted into a maternity home as a memorial to the Castleford men who died in the First World War.

The Princess Mary on the steps of the maternity home.

An inspection of the Home Guard in Carlton Street *c.*1940.

A wartime savings movement outside the Market Hall c.1942. Towns raised money to build warships and aeroplanes.

Marbles ('Taws') competitions were popular between English towns. Championships held in Castleford were known as the 'Reight Neet Aht'. Various celebrities attended and in 1940 George Formby and his wife Beryl came.

These four photographs show some of the damage inflicted in an air raid on 14 March 1941. Charles Varley of Churchfield Lane was killed in the raid. From top left to bottom right: 72-74 Churchfield Lane, 17 Churchfield Lane, 5 Hill Road and 'North View', Park Avenue.

Fourteen
Airedale and Fryston

Fryston Hall.

Fryston Hall was the home of the Milnes family until it was sold to Sir John Austin MP in 1905. The Hall was eventually demolished and provided the stone for the building of Holy Cross Church, Airedale, in 1935.

Richard Monckton Milnes of Fryston Hall was born in 1809 and was MP for Pontefract. He was created a peer in 1863, taking the title Lord Houghton. He was an author, socialite and poet. Among visitors to Fryston Hall were Disraeli and Florence Nightingale. Lord Houghton died in 1885.

Sir John Austin MP (1824-1906) was the local Member of Parliament. He resided at Redhill House (later to become the Town Hall).

In the laundry house garden at Fryston Hall.

Fryston Hall gatepost prior to 1933.

The Milnes Arms, Fryston. Popular with bargees for refreshment and the stabling of horses, it closed in February 1956 and was later demolished.

Interior view of St Peter's Church, Fryston, built in 1896 to serve the village. The building was demolished in 1991 following the closure of the colliery and migration of the community. The cemetery and war memorial remain.

Fryston village developed in the 1890's when the colliery was established. It was an isolated community with its own churches, shops and school, and also a miners welfare and sports ground with tennis courts and athletics track. Village life was captured in photographs by resident amateur photographer Jack Hulme. Many of the houses were demolished following the closure of the colliery in 1985.

Fryston Colliery Welfare sports ground c.1930's.

Copley's Farm wagon decorated for a Fryston carnival.

A large group pose in the partially built Holy Cross Church in 1934. To the left is the vicar (later Bishop), John Daly. The cubmistress (in the middle of the three uniformed ladies) is Lydia Ford. The stone came from the demolished Fryston Hall.

The Square, Airedale, shortly after completion in the late 1940's.

Airedale Methodist Church Ladies Bright Hour in the 1930's. From left to right, back row: Mmes Wallace, Owen, Lightfoot, Hancock, Coultish, Cooke, Crook, Bridges, Smith, Elliott, Burgess, Saunders, Battye, Uttley. Middle row: Mmes Aveyard, Smith, Howden, Hodgetts, Binns, Gascoigne, Nobel, Lucas, Rummins, Bowes, Dixon, Williams. Front row: Mmes Fickling, Fickling, Eddles, -?-, Parkes, Miss Henshaw, Mmes Smith, Jones, Walton, Smith.

Fifteen
Glasshoughton

Front Street, Glasshoughton c.1900.

Holywell Lane before housing development took place. To the right is Holywell Wood, which has appeared on maps since the 1820's.

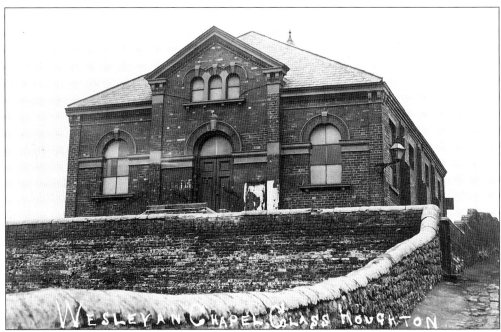

The now demolished Wesleyan Chapel at Glasshoughton which overlooked Front Street before the building of the 'glass steps'.

Rockhill, Glasshoughton *c.*1900.

A more modern view of the same area.
The Rock Inn is on the left.

An interior view of Harvey's Farm at Glasshoughton c.1890, with a profusion of furniture, ornaments and pictures.

Glasshoughton Board School in the 1880's. On the top row, second from the left, is James Henry Widdop. Girls were allowed to bring baby brothers and sisters to school when their mothers were working in the fields.

A class at Glasshoughton Board School in 1901.

A group photograph taken on Front Street, Glasshoughton, sometime between 1890 and 1910.

Two views of Glasshoughton post office and the shop of joiner and undertaker J. Tomlinson, taken sometime between 1901 and 1917.

The White House, School Lane, Glasshoughton. Originally the bearer of a thatched roof, and believed to have been in existence during the Civil War, it was owned for many years by the Carr family.

Leeds Road, looking towards the junction with Front Street. To the right is the Methodist Chapel which closed in 1986 and was later demolished. In the distance is the Wesleyan Chapel (also demolished) and buildings which stood on the site now occupied by the Castle Parade shops.

Opposite: Churchfield Lane, Glasshoughton, probably during the early part of this century.

A 1930's postcard of the Glasshoughton Coking Plant, owned by the Yorkshire Coking and Chemical Co. These cards were used as acknowledgement slips by the company.

GLASSHOUGHTON COLLIERY, SEPTEMBER 1893

Soldiers, police and colliery officials at Glasshoughton Colliery, September 1893. Troops were sent to the coalfield when a bitter strike led to unrest at Ackton Hall Colliery, Featherstone. The Riot Act was read there and two men – James Gibbs and James Duggan – were shot dead by soldiers.

Redhill Drive before housing development took place.

Acknowledgements

We would like to thank:

Mr G. Blackburn, Miss J. Brumwell, Mrs M. Jagger, Mr B.W. Pygott
and Mr R. Rockett for donations of photographs;
the editor of the *Pontefract & Castleford Express*
for permission to use photographs which appeared in that newspaper,
Mr P. Wadsworth for help and advice,
and everyone who donated or loaned photographs to Castleford Library
over the years.